MORRIS ENGEL

EARLY WORK

Interview with
Julia Van Haaften

MORRIS ENGEL

EARLY WORK

This is for Ruth,
and Mary and Andy

Catalog © 1999 Morris Engel and the Ruth Orkin Photo Archive

Photographs © 1999 Morris Engel

Published by: Ruth Orkin Photo Archive
                65 Central Park West
                New York, NY 10023
                (212) 580-1051

Web Sites: www.engelphoto.com
                www.orkinphoto.com

Designed by: Christine Zamora
Printed by: Meridian Printing, East Greenwich, Rhode Island

Front Cover: Coney Island embrace, New York City, 1938
Back Cover: Under the boardwalk, *Little Fugitive*,
                Coney Island, 1952

ISBN: 0-9676037-0-6

MORRIS ENGEL
PHOTOGRAPHER/FILMMAKER

An Interview with Julia Van Haaften

Morris Engel, 1998 Photo by Tina Ruisinger

Morris Engel's creative career defies artistic stereotyping. Fascinated by pictures since childhood, this photographer/film maker has journeyed between his two media — still photography and film — and back again, for more than sixty years. Joining the New York Photo League as a teenager in the 1930s, he also assisted on Paul Strand's film classic *Native Land*. He then photographed for the independent newspaper *PM* in the 1940s and for the US Navy during World War II. By age thirty he was a top freelancer in the golden age of magazine photography, the late 1940s and early 1950s. And Engel achieved it all before he made his first feature film, Oscar-nominated *Little Fugitive*, in 1953, which French New Wave director François Truffaut credited with revealing the possibilities of independent cinema. Engel spent the next twenty-five years making independent feature films and directing commercial film productions. Taking up a still camera again in the late 1970s he concentrated on his cherished New York City scenes until he discovered the ease and fluidity of hand-held video in the early 1990s. Though this exhibition focuses on Engel's first period of still photography, from 1935 to 1951, he feels his best work and most exciting medium is the one he's working with now — whichever that happens to be.

Self Portrait, 1936

The youngest of four children and the only son, Morris Engel was born in Williamsburg, Brooklyn in 1918 to immigrant parents from Lithuania. While still a toddler, he lost his father to tuberculosis and grew up in a feminine household, indulged and free, but also, when he was old enough, depended upon to support his widowed mother:

My interest in pictures really began when I was nine. My older sister needed some travel books for a school assignment, and I asked her friend, Willie, who knew where in Manhattan to get them, if I could go along. After a week or two of trailing along with him, I was able to do it on my own. I would get my ten cent fare, a nickel each way, start at Broadway, around the 300 block area, and walk all the way down to South Ferry, stopping at

practically every steamship company along the way, the French Line, the North German Lloyd Line, The Cunard Line, The Italian Line, and The Red Star Line. At every one I'd ask for literature, and the guy behind the counter would point to a rack and say, "Help yourself," or maybe, "Beat it, kid," knowing that I wasn't really a legitimate customer. At the end of an hour or two, I would have a pile of wonderful free books. And then, I would come home and look at them. I was very interested in pictures, and as a teenager I collected pictures that I liked, and cut them out and put them in a scrapbook.

Graduating from Lincoln High School in 1935 Engel went to work as a clerk in a banking firm to support his mother, his college goals postponed indefinitely. He feels his early experiences with pictures are directly related to his becoming a photographer at age seventeen:

I wasn't aiming to be a photographer; I was looking for something to occupy my time, and I spotted an ad in a magazine, "Photo League: Basic course $6." I said, "Boy, that sounds interesting. I can afford that." (I was making $10 a week as an office boy at the time.) I went down to the Photo League, at 31 East 21st Street, and enrolled. There were wholesale fabric shops in the neighborhood. The building itself was a brownstone walk-up, and the League was on the first floor in a large loft, with space on the walls for pictures. At the time, it was still the Film and Photo League, and some of the members of the film section were evidently much more mature and older than I was. Of course, Paul Strand and Leo Hurwitz and people like that were very important in the film section.

They became sort of advisors, almost godfathers to the Photo League. And we had other names, like Berenice Abbott and Elizabeth McCausland. The photo section was primarily young people, like myself. And the older people sort of stood out — Jim Richter, Bill Fink, Al Green. When I say older, they could have been all of — in their mid-twenties. And I can remember a man named Julian Roffman who was literally packing the materials that belonged to the film section in cardboard cartons, and that evidently was the separation of the film section from the photo section. The photo section, of course, remained at that place.

To take the Photo League course, which was given by different people under the direction of Bob Waldeck, Engel had to have a camera:

I almost acquired a camera when I was twelve years old. Eastman had a program celebrating, probably, their fiftieth anniversary, and every boy who was twelve was entitled to a free camera. Well, I was twelve. My mother and I went to the drugstore and said, "Could we have a free camera?" And they said, "No free cameras." And that ended my getting a camera when I was twelve. Told to use a film pack camera for the Photo League class, I was asked by the camera dealer whether I wanted a f.4.5 or an f.3.5. I had no idea what he was talking about, but the price was $23. And I said, "Well, that's a lot of money." But I decided to go for it.

Engel struggled first with a 9 x 12 cm camera, and then with a smaller one, called a Roland, bought mostly because he liked its Leica-like bronze finish and barrel lens:

Aaron Siskind, 1947   Photo by Morris Engel

I loved that camera's looks, but I never did get any good pictures.

The sensitizing and enlightening influence of growing up the only male in a female household cannot be overestimated in appreciating Engel's gentle humanism nor in understanding his open-hearted artistic embrace:

At the beginning, just to see how I'd get an image on film, I would shoot the people easiest and closest to me — my mother at home, my sister, and so on. I did endless pictures of my mother just to see what an exposure was like, how to process film, and how to make a print. I used the Photo League darkrooms at first, but later on I set up a primitive darkroom at home. There was an Elwood enlarger, which cost something like $10, or maybe $15. It was a large wooden enlarger. Then I went to a pawn shop and got an anastigmat lens, and that cost another five bucks, and then trays, etc. Now in order to use the darkness, I would wait until the night time and then my work would begin, making the pictures.

PM Photo Staff, (Morris, second from left)

Within a year I became involved in what was probably the best group I could have joined, the feature group led by Aaron Siskind. He was older, probably ten years our senior, and he was a teacher in the public school system. He got together a group of "kids" — Harold Corsini, Jack Manning, Saul Prom, Lucy Ashjian — and almost instantly the group started functioning, making pretty decent pictures of different projects we were working on. One was "Harlem Document." Another was Park Avenue: North and South; another was the Bowery, and a couple of others. But primarily we concentrated on one project at a time. It was an extremely valuable learning place for me, and I think for almost everyone involved. The feature group became the example of how to make pictures. Shortly thereafter other groups of the Photo League came into being, and they shot Pitt Street and some of the other projects. I realized that there were a lot of important names attached to the Photo League, and eventually almost all the major photo names were either connected to the Photo League or showed at the Photo League: Ansel Adams, Edward Weston, Paul Strand, Weegee, Lewis Hine, Gene Smith, Bob Frank, and so on.

The Museum of Modern Art in those days had two wonderful features. You'd go up to the fourth floor, and just walk into the library. No admission charge, no appointments necessary. And I would go to their photo section, and from their racks, I would take down the annuals, the photo annuals...British, French, German...I think the Americans were just starting. But I would thumb through every page and look at the different pictures. It was my self-education in the kind of photography I liked. This was actually from 1935 and '36. It could have been a little earlier, but that's close. I just loved photography. In addition, the museum showed a foreign movie every day, and here again, it was free, no appointments. And I got a tremendous education in foreign movies because in those days there were only a couple of houses in the city that showed foreign films. One was on 14th, and the other was on 42nd Street. The museum was free, and it was wonderful.

One day at the Photo League, I met a friend who had a Rollei (Rolleiflex), and I asked to borrow it. I was working in Harlem at the time for the feature group, and the very first day with that camera I took one of the best pictures I've ever made, called Harlem Merchant, a man behind a small corner candy stand (see page 13). After that picture, I realized that the Rolleiflex was my camera, and for the rest of my life it was very special. I remember walking on 21st Street, and saying to myself, "Lewis Hine walked on this very street." I said to myself, "Well, you're going to be great photographer." And I had absolutely not even a concept of what it meant.

At the Photo League, in addition to the pioneering documentarian Lewis Hine (1874-1940), Engel met

Paul Strand (1890-1976) whose revolutionary "straight photography" in the 1910s set a direction for American photographers for the rest of the century. Strand was also one of the founders of Frontier Films, the documentary group formed by several ex-film members of the Film and Photo League. He took an interest in Engel and asked him if he would like to learn how to make movies as an assistant (unpaid) on his next film. Though Engel had recently lost his job at the brokerage, he summoned the financial courage to accept:

He said go out and practice without film. So I took the very heavy camera and tripod. I felt very uncomfortable and practiced without film. It immediately attracted attention, and people would stop and look at the camera. I shot for a couple of days. I was really impatient, I said "Can I shoot with film now?" Strand said, "Okay." We went to a couple of different places, and I shot different scenes. At the end of the day, we looked at the rushes in a screening room next to the lab in the Film Center at 630 Ninth Avenue. And, if Strand said, "Morris, that's good," I just glowed. In the finished film, Native Land (1942), there are twenty seconds of the footage I shot. And, because the credits read "Photography by Paul Strand," I considered that the ultimate compliment, that my stuff was good enough for him to put his name on. And that was my introduction to movies. I've always felt that to be a good movie maker, you should do still photography first. And, I've always felt that to be a good still photographer, you should do movies first. Now, of course the question is which to

PM Cover, 1940   Photo By Morris Engel

do first — I don't think it matters too much, but in the history of photography, there haven't been many people who have done both.

In 1939 Morris Engel had a solo exhibition at the New School for Social Research. Paul Strand contributed the exhibition's introduction (see page 11):

I felt that Strand was doing something wonderful for me, and when I thanked him, he said, "I wasn't just doing it for you." What he was doing was writing a history of straight photography and specifically the Photo League. And it was possibly because Stieglitz or Hine did that for him. It's an interesting correlation.

After his solo exhibition, Engel approached Ralph Steiner, the photo editor of Marshall Field's national daily newspaper, PM, which began in June 1940 and

Self Portrait, 1945

sold for five cents when the *New York Daily News* or *The New York Times* cost two:

I said, "Do you have any interest in these pictures?" and before I knew it, my photographs were in the Sunday Gallery, which was several full pages in their Sunday magazine section. It was the best possible platform. And in a little while, because of that spread, I got a couple of assignments. For example, at the opening of the school year, he asked me to go out and take pictures of school kids on opening day, and I did and then called the office. He said, "Well, while you're there, see if you can shoot a couple of pictures of what the girls are wearing for our fashion section." So I finished that, and called him, and he said, "On your way back, stop at this school, see if you can get this picture," and I did that. The next day several photos were used. And in a little while, the head of the photo department, Harry Baker, asked, "Engel, how would you like to be on the staff?" I said, "Yes." He said, "Will you work for 35?" Even though I knew that the older guys were making close to 60. So I said, yes. He returns

shortly afterward and says, "I can't pay you 35! I've got to pay you 40. That's the guild minimum." From that moment on I would find myself spending a day, or an afternoon, with Jascha Heifitz, or Ingrid Bergman, or Babe Ruth. And that was unbelievable.

When I joined PM I didn't really know how to handle the Speed Graphic which was the basic camera for their staff. I tried later on to use a Rollei, but basically the camera was the Speed Graphic. PM *had a small waiting room for photography, and the assignment editor was Baker, then Sally Pepper who was one of the better known assignment editors. They would read* The New York Times *or get other information from press people, and they would say, "Morris, cover this, this, this." And there would just be endless daily experiences. For example, I'm in the photo room waiting for an assignment, and Sally says, "Morris, grab your camera. There's a man hanging from his fingertips from the Manhattan Bridge." The Manhattan Bridge, where...in any event, I'm halfway out the door. She says, "Make that the Brooklyn Bridge!" And it was one of those ridiculous situations. But* PM *was truly a wonderful amazing place for me to learn and to enjoy life. The assignments and the experiences were wonderful, and* PM *was the only paper in those days that gave photographers a credit line. So if I took a picture, and it appeared in the paper the next day, it would say "Photo by Morris Engel." Weegee got famous from his credit line on* PM; *if you worked for the News or the Times, you didn't get credit, and no one would know you. I'm sure there were loads of very talented guys on the other papers, but no one knows them now.*

So, I would get credit and life was wonderful. You get confidence, respect and experience as a staff photographer, especially on a paper like PM.

Sooner or later, I had an idea that America was going to become involved in the war. And even though working on the paper was wonderful, I had the feeling that it wasn't going to last long. The PM guys who had a college degree entered the Army as officers. I had no degree, and it was uncertain where I would end up in the Army, certainly not as an officer. But if I joined the Navy, I could become a photographer immediately because I knew the people involved in the photo section. And they said, "Sure, join us, and we'll put you here." So I joined the Navy, and I immediately entered as a one-stripe photographer's first mate. As a Navy photographer, I was on practically every type of ship the Navy had, from Coast Guard cutters to World War I destroyers, making the North Atlantic crossing from New York to Europe, being on troop transports, on cruisers, on PT boats, and even on aircraft carriers.

Well, we landed in London and I became a member of the Combat Photo Unit #8 because I had a news photographer's background. I knew that our basic objective was to cover the European invasion, D-Day in Normandy. I ended up on the beach called Utah. And Capt. Edward Steichen, who was in charge of all Navy photography, signed a citation saying that I was in Normandy on D-Day, and I did this and this and this. And now it's an important part of my life. After that, we went down to cover the invasion in the south France area. I was asked to volunteer for picket boat duty, and I accepted, knowing full well that the

U.S. Navy, South France, 1944

picket boat was the director of traffic for the first wave attacking the enemy. I really thought that my life was definitely going to be ended in the next few hours.

After the south France action I ended up back in London, and then was transferred to Anacostia where eventually I became a chief, which changed the uniform I was wearing. And after being chief, I was discharged from the service.

PM was a dying operation, losing money and circulation. I came in one day, and found a notice from the editor, John Lewis, "Dear Morris, we love you, but goodbye." They fired 42 people that day. The Newspaper Guild fought the firings, and publisher Ralph Ingersoll said, "Okay, we'll take three people back." I was one of the three, but I said, "No. You fired me, and I'm not going back," and fortunately, I didn't.

Yank Cover, 1944   Photo by Morris Engel

When the Photo League was listed on the subversive list, of course, that was a tremendous blow and a terrible time for everyone connected with the League. Just after PM *and I separated, somebody said, "Morris, I know the editor of the* Ladies Home Journal. *How would you like to be introduced to her?" I said, "*Ladies Home Journal! *Are you kidding!" I was so ignorant, I didn't realize that the* Journal *and* McCall's *had some of the best photography in those days. It was really the golden age of magazine photography.*

Having a lot of free time allowed Engel to explore picture stories on his own. One concerned a Lower East Side shoeshine boy and another a girl in Harlem. Linking these and his later magazine narratives with Engel's early films is their unsentimental evocation of childhood's vivid emotional landscape:

I saw a kid shining shoes on 14th Street. I found he lived on East 10th Street. I met his parents, "Look, I'd like to do some pictures, you know." There would be no charge. And there won't be any problems. So they said okay. And I worked for probably a week or two, just shooting pictures of this boy named Fred, as a shoeshine kid, as a school kid, part of a family, and his life on the street. Just about this time I did a story about a little girl, Rebecca, and her two sisters and mother, living in a relatively low-grade apartment in Harlem.

I decided I would show [Freddy's story] to different editors. One of the editors I called was John Morris, photo editor of the Ladies Home Journal. *I said, "I've got a picture story I'd like to show you." He said, could he buy it? I said, "Of course you can buy it." And that was my first contact with the* Ladies Home Journal. *They did a layout, and I think I got $1,000. And then they offered me their choice assignment, "How America Lives." A photographer would be sent for a week or two to all parts of the country, living with a family, and just shooting pictures of whatever actions took place within that family framework. So I would do a story for John...somebody in Chicago, somebody in Albany, somebody in Idaho, somebody in Texas, somebody in Seattle, Washington. They were wonderful assignments. And the more I did, the easier it became for me to get assignments with the other magazines, because it was a great showcase.*

Now, I had actually lived with a photo editor, a guy named John Peter, in London when I was in the Navy. He was the photo editor of McCall's. *I could never get an assignment with him, but after the* Ladies Home Journal *articles started to come out, he said, "Morris, do this, this." I said, "Fine." He sent me to Chicago, and there was a top writer named John Bartlow Martin. And I did a couple stories with him there, the back-of-the-yards type stories, etc. And then,* Fortune, Collier's, This Week, *all the other magazines became easier and easier as I was doing more and more photography work. And it would simply be phoning the editors, knowing that...or them knowing that I did the How America Lives stories and seeing the results. (*Fortune *used to send me to Harvard so often I felt Harvard owed me a degree.)*

I joined a photo co-op called Scope Associates. Scope was a group of a half a dozen top photographers. They had an office on 41st and Second Avenue. And I joined them because I thought it would make life a little easier for me in terms of billing, in terms of prices and so on. And they had top people there, like Fons Ianelli, Victor Jorgenson, Lisa Larson, George Heyer, and Mike Ehrenberg and tremendous technicians, Charlie Reiche, a darkroom genius. They had a director. They had some pretty big names as members, and most of the photography of the Scope people was for the top magazines, Ladies Home Journal, McCall's, Fortune, Collier's *and so on, at top prices. And it was just a wonderful kind of experience.*

Yet, while I was doing all this work, I realized that the assignments were getting fewer and fewer. Meanwhile, I became friends with a man I had met in the Navy named Charlie Woodruff. He was really a mechanical genius. He built a custom 35mm movie camera for me,

Morris, 1947

designed to be handheld, which eventually became the heart and soul of why Little Fugitive *was possible.*

And that is another story for another time . . .

New York City, October 2, 1999
Interview with Julia Van Haaften

Curator of Photographs
Miriam and Ira D. Wallach Division of Art,
Prints & Photographs
The New York Public Library

MORRIS ENGEL'S EXHIBITION AT THE NEW SCHOOL, 1939

By Paul Strand

Morris Engel's photographs are both important in themselves and as a part of a vital development in American Photography. In the past four or five years the tradition, of which Lewis Hine is the outstanding pioneer, has received a strong new impulse that has brought fresh air into the stale atmosphere of a very empty photographic pictorialism. An ever growing number of photographers, many of them still young, have turned their cameras upon their environment and have begun to document both America and the time in which they themselves live. People, people on the land and in the cities, the vast social physiognomy of American, this has been the point of focus. Photographers have turned their eyes and the "eye of the camera" upon human suffering and need, upon human dignity and courage. The resulting photographs, for want of a better word, have been called "documentary." Their value does not lie in the word, but in the fact that they direct our attention, our thought and our understanding toward those urgent problems which America through the New Deal has only begun to face and to solve.

This group of photographers who have become magnetized to the pressing demands of their own world and of their own land, becomes ever larger. The use of the camera as an instrument of investigation, of record, and of communication, has already produced an invaluable body of work. Outstanding contributors have been Dorothea Lange, Ben Shahn and other members of the staff of the Farm Security Administration: Margaret Bourke-White's and Erskine Caldwell's, "You Have Seen Their Faces"; the work of the W.P.A. projects; and in New York the production by the Photo League, not only of photographs, but of photographers. For the Photo League, now numbering seventy members, has been a center in which many young and talented photographers have received their training, where they have been able to get both technical knowledge as well as a contact with the whole historical development of photography as a medium of expression.

Morris Engel, after four years of work at the Photo League, comes forward with a group of photographs which are of the greatest interest. Here is a young man of twenty-one who sees people with compassionate understanding, as they move within the city's tumult or relax for a few hours at a nearby beach. Great particularity characterizes his most successful photographs. Inasmuch as generalization has been a characteristic weakness of documentary photography, this is a step forward. Engel sees his subjects very specifically and intensely. They are not types, but people in whom the quality of the life they live is vivid—unforgettable. And by the quickness of his vision not of his shutter, he has been able to seize this expressiveness of the person as he or she moves down an avenue or street, amid the welter of city movement. Sometimes it is not one person but several whom he photographs; a man glancing at a girl as he goes into a subway; a group of people on a park bench, or a family out for a walk. Here, too, the portraiture is held with the additional element of an attempt to photograph relationships between people. This last is perhaps the most vital and interesting quality which distinguishes Mr. Engel's work. It is one which has infinite possibilities for development. His unusual capacity not only to see keenly and quickly, but also to integrate plastically what he sees gives promise of an important contribution to photography. This, his first one-man show, is in itself solid evidence of genuine talent. ■

Paul Strand at Work, New Jersey, 1947

Harlem Merchant, New York City, 1937

Picket Line, New York City, 1937

Mother and Daughter, "Back of the Yards", Chicago, 1949

Park Avenue, New York City, 1938

Shopping, Ninth Avenue, New York City, 1938

Shoeshine Boy with Cop, 14th Street, New York City, 1947

Shoeshine Boy, New York City, 1947

Shoeshine Boy on East 10th Street, New York City, 1947

Scooter, Trenton, New Jersey, 1947

Rebecca Holding On, New York City, 1947

Two Women, Lower East Side, 1938

Joe Palooka, New York City, 1946

Smoking, Coney Island, 1938

Women on the Beach, Coney Island, 1938

Beach Trio, Coney Island, 1938

Water Fountain, Coney Island, 1938

Drying Off, Coney Island, 1938

Beach Play, Coney Island, 1938

New Shoes, "Back of the Yards", Chicago, 1949

Race, Lower East Side, 1936

Rebecca, Harlem, 1947

Couple at Horse Auction, Williamsburg, Brooklyn, 1947

Sweet Evelyn, New York City, 1938

Martha, New York City, 1948

Boy Crying, Harlem, 1936

Mother's Profile, Trenton, New Jersey, 1947

Sweet Potato Peddler, New York City, 1938

Puppet Show, New York City, 1947

Newsstand Comics, New York City, 1946

Street Shower, New York City, 1938

Circus Poster, New York City, 1946

CHRONOLOGY

1918	Born April 8 in New York City
1935	Joined the Photo League
1939	Solo exhibition, The New School; worked on film *Native Land* with Paul Strand
1940	Staff photographer, *PM* newspaper
1941-45	U.S. Navy, Chief Photographer's Mate, Combat Photo Unit #8,
1945-47	Resumed work as staff photographer on *PM*
1947-51	Freelance work for magazines: *Ladies Home Journal, McCall's, Collier's, Fortune, This Week,* and others
1951	Made 35mm motion picture short, *The Farm They Won*
1952	Co-produced, co-directed, co-writer and photographed *Little Fugitive,* award-winning feature film
1952	Married Ruth Orkin
1955	Co-produced, co-directed, co-writer and photographed *Lovers and Lollipops,* award-winning feature film
1958	Produced, directed and photographed *Weddings and Babies,* award-winning feature film
1960	Did CBS television story on Brasilia
1961	Corporate film for Chase Manhattan Bank
1961-66	Directed television commercials, including award-winning Oreos commercial
1962	*The Dog Lover,* a film starring Jack Guilford
1968	*I Need a Ride to California,* 35mm color feature film; "Peace Is," short color film
1994	Video feature *A Little Bit Pregnant*
1998	Video feature *Camellia*

AWARDS

United States Navy Photographic Institute Citation for Exceptionally Meritorious Photography, Awarded Navy Day, October 27, 1945

For outstanding achievement while serving as a U.S. Navy Combat photographer and as a member of combat photo unit number eight. For an exceptionally fine series of still photographs of the invasions in Southern France and on the Normandy Beaches, where his indifference to danger and his keen awareness of what scenes were most vital in the action around him, resulted in a contribution of great value to the visual records of the war. His photograph showing enemy dead on the Normandy beach, taken on D-day and in the face of grave danger, is one of the great pictures of the war and reflects the highest credit upon Engel and the U.S. Navy photographic service.

Signed by Edward Steichen, Captain USNR/Director, Navy Photographic Institute

Mayor's Office of Film, Theatre and Broadcasting, Crystal Apple Award, 1988

Lifetime Achievement Award, Photographic Administrators, 1998